HOW THEY LIVED

The
ROMANS

NEIL GRANT

MALLARD PRESS

The Roman baths in Bath, England. The Romans carried their advanced, urban civilization to countries which would not reach similar standards of material comfort for a thousand years after the Romans had left.

Contents

Introduction

In 700 B.C. Rome was nothing more than a group of peasant villages on the River Tiber. From them grew one of the greatest empires the world has ever seen.

About 615 B.C. the Etruscans, a more advanced people, took over the settlements on the Tiber and the first city was built. After about 100 years of Etruscan rule, the leading Romans rebelled and set up their own republic, with some degree of democratic government. For the next 200 years the small republic was almost constantly at war with the Etruscans and other neighbours. By 300 B.C. it was the strongest power in Italy.

Rome's greatest early rival in the region was Carthage, in North Africa. In spite of the exploits of Hannibal, a Carthaginian general who invaded Italy by crossing the Alps with an army that included elephants, Carthage itself was completely destroyed by the Romans by 202 B.C.

Rome was then unchallenged in the western Mediterranean, but the Republic itself was in trouble. After a period of civil war and dictatorship, the army became the main influence in politics, and Rome became the prize to be gained by the most successful Roman general.

In 46 B.C. Julius Caesar, who had won a great reputation by his conquests in Gaul (France), seized supreme power. He proved a wise ruler, who ended the upper-class gang warfare that Roman politics had become, but he was assassinated in 44 B.C. by a group of patricians (noblemen) who feared that he was about to create an hereditary monarchy.

That, in fact, is what happened. From the power struggle that followed Caesar's murder, his adopted son Octavian emerged the victor. He became the first Roman emperor (27 B.C.–A.D. 14), taking the name Augustus.

Republican traditions remained, but the emperor held supreme power. Augustus himself was an able ruler, but the same could not be said of his immediate successors. One was certainly insane; two acted as if they were. After the Emperor Nero was driven out in A.D. 68, the title of emperor became again a prize to be won by Rome's most favoured general.

This actually turned out to be a great improvement. Under a succession of honourable rulers, the Roman Empire enjoyed peace and prosperity for over 100 years. This *pax Romana* ("Roman peace") was perhaps the greatest achievement of Roman civilization.

The Emperor Hadrian (A.D. 117–138) inherited the empire when it was at its largest. It covered about 2,500,000 square miles and stretched from Scotland to Syria, and included all the lands around the Mediterranean.

Hadrian, however, deliberately reduced the size of the empire. Certain far-distant provinces were not worth holding on to because of the cost of defending them. This was a wise policy, the immediate effects of which were peace and prosperity. But it was also a sign of the times.

After Hadrian the empire was almost always on the defensive. The Roman legions no longer fought to conquer new provinces, but fought to hold on to what they had. In the 3rd century, when economic problems added to Rome's difficulties, the empire entered on its long, inevitable decline.

For a thousand years after the fall of the empire, Roman civilization remained a model for all of Europe. Even the title of "Holy Roman Emperor" ("Holy" meaning Christian) was revived. Roman ideas and institutions were thought (in some ways correctly) as superior to those of other societies. Latin, the language of the Romans, was the common language of educated Europeans until the 16th century, and was still a compulsory subject for university students in the mid-20th century.

The Roman Empire was a truly international civilization. "Roman" came to mean all respectable citizens – not just those born in Rome; several emperors were of foreign birth. It included people of many races, languages and religions, who were united by shared institutions, especially Roman law and the Latin language. Roman ideas and methods – for example in building – were adopted throughout the empire and also influenced people outside it. The Roman Empire was smaller than some empires that have arisen since. But although it might not have been the largest, it was probably the greatest and most successful.

Roman mosaic from the Piazza Armerina in Sicily.

Government and People

Sovereignty of the People?

On the monuments of ancient Rome and on the banners of the Roman legions, these letters appeared: SPQR. They stood for the Latin words meaning "For the Roman Senate and People". This remained the motto of Rome long after the old republic had disappeared and when supreme power belonged not to the people or the Senate, but to the emperor. The Romans, nevertheless, always remembered their republican traditions, and the idea that authority depended on the will of the people never died. It became, though, just an idea, with no practical effect.

In the Republic, the citizens expressed their will in various assemblies, but the laws were made and government was controlled by the Senate. The Senate was an assembly of the most powerful men (originally, 100 of them; by Augustus's time, 600). At the head of the government there were the two consuls, who were elected every year.

Increasingly, however, power fell into the hands of a few powerful families. As the empire expanded, and rich Romans became even richer, quarrels between the patrician, or aristocratic, class and the ordinary people became more bitter. After a century of troubles, the republic finally disappeared altogether. Yet when Octavian (soon to be the Emperor Augustus) came to power, his first act was to appear to restore the institutions of the republic.

This was, however, just for show. Elections were still held, but the emperor said who was to be elected. He was really a dictator, though Augustus was a wise and (by the standards of the time) a reasonably kindly one. The real power of the emperor and his successors rested on the army. The Senate could sometimes influence events, but it had no real authority. This system of power collapsed in A.D. 69 when Augustus died without leaving an heir. It was the legions who now made their favourite general, Vespasian, emperor.

Opposite: This map of the Roman Empire at its height (3rd century A.D.) show its vast extent – from the borders of Scotland in the west to Syria in the east.

Right: Cicero, one of the day's leading politicians, addressing the Senate.

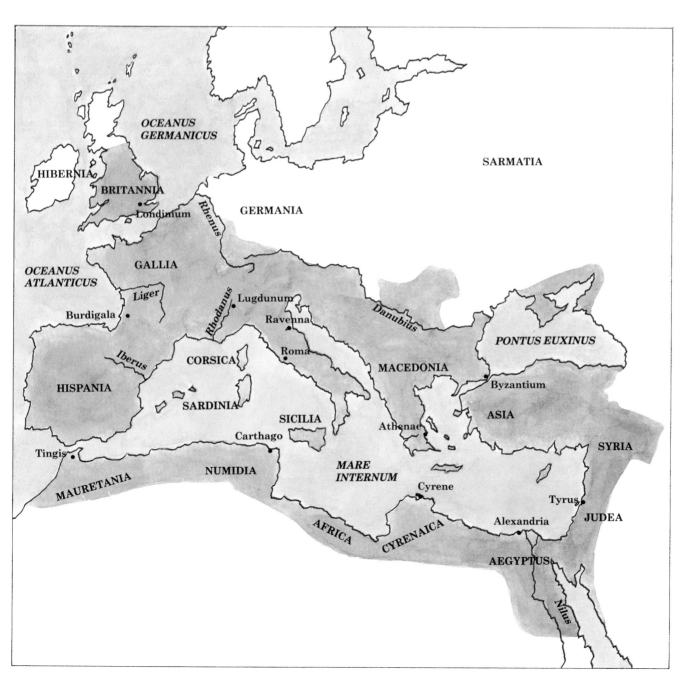

OCEANUS
GERMANICUS

SARMATIA

HIBERNIA

BRITANNIA

• Londinium

GERMANIA

OCEANUS
ATLANTICUS

GALLIA

Liger

Rhenus

Danubius

PONTUS EUXINUS

Burdigala •

Rhodanus

Lugdunum •

Ravenna •

Iberus

CORSICA

Roma •

MACEDONIA

Byzantium

HISPANIA

SARDINIA

ASIA

SICILIA

Athenae

SYRIA

Tingis •

Carthago •

MARE
INTERNUM

MAURETANIA

NUMIDIA

Cyrene •

Tyrus •

JUDEA

AFRICA

CYRENAICA

Alexandria •

AEGYPTUS

Nilus

9

A figure of a Roman lictor carrying the symbols of the consul's authority.

Public Service

An upper-class Roman considered it his duty to serve the state, and there were a

range of official posts by which, like civil servants today, he rose up the political ladder. The first objective was to become a senator, but before he reached that stage he had to serve in various other posts, starting off as a *quaestor*, who was in charge of local taxation and other financial administration. He also had to own property of at least a certain value.

He had reached the top when he was appointed *consul*. There were two consuls, holding office for one year, with supreme authority under the emperor. They were accompanied by twelve *lictors*, who carried a bundle of rods and an axe, symbols of the consul's power. The consuls opened debates in the Senate and proposed new laws. When their year of office was over, they usually then went on to become governor of a province.

Roman senators, who were appointed for life, held a variety of different jobs in the course of their careers. At an early stage they would probably have done some military service. They were also lawyers, magistrates and administrators. As a consul or a provincial governor, they also held a military command and led the army in battle.

Government positions were subject to keen competition. Romans were ambitious, and even when they were acting as little more than instruments for carrying out the emperor's orders, they still had some power of their own – and the opportunity to make money. One way or another, a man usually ended his spell as a provincial governor much richer than he was when he started. His wealth might come from keeping a share of the money paid in taxes or by other doubtful means. Such means of making money were usually accepted by the public. On the whole the public servants of the empire carried out their duties efficiently and sensibly. Some parts of Europe enjoyed more reasonable government under the Romans than they would experience for centuries after the empire had fallen.

The Provinces

When the Romans conquered a new province, their aim was to adapt it to Roman government as swiftly as possible. Local customs were tolerated as long as they did not conflict with Roman ways of life. There was no point in upsetting people needlessly: a hostile population only involved Rome in extra expense.

In a province such as Britain for example, Roman customs were adopted by the local people very quickly, despite the early harsh rule which provoked the rebellion of Boudicca (Boadicea). Intelligent people, who already knew something of Roman ways, could see many advantages in the *pax Romana*. Perhaps that did not reconcile them to the Roman conquest, but by the time their children grew up, Roman rule was accepted as natural. People had learned to speak Latin and wear the toga. Some of them became Roman citizens, and they were proud of it.

The Emperor Hadrian tried to make the empire less expensive to defend by giving up distant, troublesome provinces and improving defences. He ordered the construction of a fortified wall in northern Britain, between the estuaries of the rivers Tyne and Solway, to keep out the raiding Picts.

11

Right: Part of the Roman forum, with the remains of the temple of Castor and Pollux. In many provincial towns, the forum or a forum (there were sometimes more than one) was also the market place. Shops, large and small, were grouped around it.

Opposite: The standard garment of the well-to-do Roman citizen was the toga, a piece of cloth (usually wool) about 6 m (20 ft) long which was draped around the body in a complicated way – the wearer needed a slave to help him arrange it. It was gathered at the waist by a girdle and the long end thrown over the left shoulder. A fold of the toga could also serve as a hat.

Roman Law

The Roman Empire was bound together not by the might of Roman armies (though they certainly had a part to play) so much as by Roman law and the Roman language.

Roman law is the foundation of the legal system of all Western countries. In the early years of the Republic, certain laws and punishments had been laid down, and these were kept as a kind of backbone to the law. As one lawyer defined it, law is "the art of the good and the fair". The Romans, stern governors in many ways, approached the law as a matter of common sense. Much of it was built up from precedent – what had been done before – that is, on the decisions of magistrates and judges in previous cases, and on the edicts issued by the *praetors*. The praetors were the officials in charge of administering the law, and they held office for a year. Praetors as well as other magistrates relied on the advice of legal experts.

The great strength of Roman law was that, although it could be harsh, it was generally fair. Penalties were severe; not all magistrates were honest and just, or even intelligent. But for the most part people recognized that the law was just, and they were therefore willing to accept it. The Romans understood very well that a law which is resented by most of the people it governs is as bad as no law at all.

In the provinces, governors generally left local affairs to local magistrates. As long as law and order were maintained, and taxes were paid on time, justice could be left to the natives.

Citizens and Others

The law, however, was not applied equally to everyone. It was, for example, an advantage to be a Roman citizen. Originally, this meant only property-owning residents of Rome, but it was later extended, first to other Italian cities, then to cities outside Italy, and finally to most free men living within the empire.

Citizenship had many advantages. It was, for instance, easier to engage in trade and business if you were a citizen. A citizen was more likely to receive favourable treatment if he got into trouble with the authorities. As we read in the Bible, St. Paul was once arrested and about to be flogged when he asked the official if it was right to treat a Roman citizen in such a way. The official, who had not realized St. Paul was a Roman citizen, hurriedly released him.

The inhabitants of an average town in the Roman Empire included citizens, free men who were not (or not yet) citizens, and a variety of others, such as merchants and travellers whose homes were in another town or province. They might also include

Prisoners-of-war became slaves. This rather crude carving from Trier in Germany shows two captives being dragged off in chains.

army veterans, who often colonized new towns built near the frontiers to guard against barbarian attack and to set a good example.

In some towns, but especially in Rome itself, there were also many slaves. Slavery existed in all ancient civilizations, but it would be wrong to compare it to the kind of slavery which existed in the southern states of the U.S.A. before the Civil War. Most slaves were prisoners of war, captured during the Roman campaigns of conquest. Others were bought from outside the empire, but these too were usually the losers in some distant tribal war.

Although slaves were the property of their master and had practically no legal rights themselves, they were often treated no worse than ordinary servants and sometimes like members of the family. More important, perhaps, they were not condemned to be slaves for ever. Some became skilled craftsmen, even doctors; they could buy their freedom or they could be granted it by their masters. On the other hand there were many cases of extreme cruelty to slaves, which provoked rebellions among the slave-labour force in southern Italy.

While slaves could, and often did, become free men, free men could also become slaves, though less often. Sometimes a man would sell himself into slavery in order to pay his debts.

This kind of slavery was one sign of the flexibility of Roman society. It is easy to think of the Romans as rather rigid people, but in fact there was a good deal of movement up and down the social scale. Not all senators by any means belonged to the old patrician class, and it was possible for a man of humble birth in the provinces to rise to a high position in Rome. Two of the last Roman emperors were born in Spain, while one came from Africa.

Towns

The Romans were tremendous builders, not only in Rome itself but all over their huge empire. When Augustus became emperor, there was hardly a stone-built city in Europe. Within 200 years it was dotted with them, from Yorkshire to Syria.

When a new town was built, it was planned in advance by surveyors. These men were highly trained and good ones were hard to find. The younger Pliny, when he was governor of the province of Bythnia, tried to get some surveyors from Rome, but the emperor wrote back to say he was short of surveyors himself and Pliny would have to find his own locally.

Besides planning the towns and directing their construction, the surveyors were also responsible for the land around the towns. This land provided food for the townsfolk as well as giving the town itself an income from rents or rates.

The town was planned on the grid system – streets running at right angles. Near the centre was the forum, the main square, surrounded by colonnades and shops, a general meeting place where people exchanged gossip, discussed business and (perhaps) sometimes hatched plots. On one side of the forum was a large hall-like building called a basilica where the town council met and the magistrates held court. Even the smallest town had its public baths and temples. There might also be a theatre and other public buildings such as an athletics stadium or a "circus" or hippodrome for chariot racing.

The remains of a Roman street in the south Italian city of Pompeii, preserved by the volcanic eruption which buried it. Though Roman towns were spacious, minor streets were rather narrow, and often became so crowded that it was difficult to walk down them.

The great building
projects of the
Romans were powered
mainly by muscles, as
in this picture of
slaves on a treadmill.

Rome

Rome, of course, was different. Like great cities of any age, it was a place of striking contrasts. On the one hand were the splendid palaces, temples, triumphal arches, baths and other grand marble buildings, a few of which are still standing today. On the other hand there were crowded slums and narrow streets where it was almost impossible to make one's way through the stalls of tradesmen and crowds of people.

There was a huge gap between rich and poor. Rich men grew even richer by buying up large estates when land was cheap. The land was then worked by slave labour, while the peasants who had lived there joined the poor of Rome. Their sense of duty often made rich men devote some of their wealth to public projects or to charity; in this way the prosperity of the wealthy was passed into the rest of society. However, such acts of charity did not reduce their highly luxurious living standards, nor did they bring an end to the poverty of the masses of unemployed – peasants without land and craftsmen who could not find work because their jobs were done by slaves.

At the same time, the ordinary people of Rome were proud, assertive and aware of the rights which they had gained under the Republic. They could not be ignored.

In fact, Rome often seemed ready to explode into revolution. But the emperors and nobility were well aware of the danger. They attempted to keep the masses contented, for instance, by gifts of free corn or by keeping prices down by subsidies. Wise emperors like Hadrian were careful not to make too much of the imperial cult (in which the emperor himself was worshipped as a god) in Rome itself, for fear of offending the people.

Rome was often alive with rumours of plots, of defeats in war, or murders in high places. Panic and riot were easily provoked. It was always necessary – or at least desirable – to keep a large detachment of soldiers near the city in case the Romans themselves had to be brought under control.

With perhaps a million inhabitants, Rome was intensely crowded and, inevitably, noisy and dirty. It was therefore sub-

ject to the disasters that have plagued all big cities up to recent times. The first of these was fire.

In the reign of the Emperor Nero (A.D. 54–68), a terrible fire destroyed much of Rome, burning for a week. Some said the Emperor himself started the fire, others blamed it on the Christians, but it was probably an accident. The historian Tacitus wrote a vivid account of that terrible week, when some people, having lost everything, preferred to die in the fire instead of escaping. But although this was probably the worst fire in ancient Rome, it was not the only one. Augustus had organized a fire brigade after a fire in A.D. 5, though it was obviously incapable of dealing with a major outbreak.

One disaster sometimes causes another. Italy is subject to earthquakes, which causes floods, sending people to the tops of the highest buildings to escape. The damage and destruction left behind allowed disease to flourish. One casualty was the Emperor Marcus Aurelius, who died in an epidemic of smallpox in A.D. 180.

The remains of Trajan's Market in Rome. The arcades held shops and craftsmen's workshops.

Family Life

Houses

Rome was the first city to have blocks of flats. Space was so scarce that it was cheaper to build upwards. But these blocks were strictly for the poorer people. The buildings were shoddy and likely to collapse, and the apartments nearer the top (the largest had five or six storeys) had no water or heating – nothing more than walls, floor and ceiling. As several Romans complained, when you were walking the streets you were lucky if nothing worse than a bucket of slops fell on your head.

Those who lived in these blocks were also in severe danger of fire.

The common type of house in Rome, which, with variations, existed throughout the empire, was a house or villa with two standard features called the *atrium* and the *peristyle*. The atrium was an open courtyard and the peristyle a garden surrounded by a portico, or colonnade, rather like cloisters in a monastery, at the back of the house. The other rooms – dining room, bedrooms, kitchen, sometimes a bathroom – were grouped around it. From the outside these villas looked rather plain. Inside they were luxurious, with rich wall paintings and (after about A.D. 100) mosaic floors.

Colonnades and courtyards made Roman villas attractive and elegant dwellings. This is the House of the Vettii in Pompeii.

The Family

The Romans took family life seriously. Roman writers were always complaining that family life was not what it used to be in the good old days of the Republic, and many of the more responsible emperors tried to encourage the idea of the family, even penalizing people who reached a certain age without getting married.

Family life was no less important than duty to the state. In fact, the two were connected. The family was, in Roman eyes, like the state in miniature, and unless families prospered, the state would not either. There was a good deal of truth in this idea: the decline of family life in the later years of the empire happened at the same time as the decline of the empire itself.

The family group, at least among the better-off, was a large one. Besides man, wife and children, there were other relations, and people with no blood relationship who were dependent on the father of the family in some way and were treated as members of the household. The slaves too belonged to the household.

Obviously, the members of the household were of widely differing rank. But over all of them the father of the family, *pater familias*, ruled much as the emperor ruled over the state. He was a dictator, kind (usually) but stern. The great writer Cicero said a man whom he regarded as an ideal father ruled and directed his household, was feared by his slaves, respected by his children, and loved by everyone.

A new-born child did not become a member of the family until it was accepted by the father. He could order it to be "exposed" – left to die on a rubbish dump – if he did not want it.

The Roman matron, wife and mother, was also a person who commanded great respect. Roman history and literature is full of stories of loyal and devoted mothers. Her main job was to run the household. There were slaves to do the chores, though she would take part in traditional women's

work such as spinning yarn from wool.

As in most societies, the relationship between man and wife depended as much on the character of the individuals concerned as on custom and law, but there was no doubt that a wife had to obey her husband. He was even entitled, legally, to kill her if she were unfaithful, though such a thing seldom happened. We hear more of bossy wives than oppressed ones, although that does not prove that many women were not oppressed.

Marriages were usually arranged rather than happen by chance. Considerations of property and social standing were more important than love. Although most marriages seem to have been happy, some men were unfaithful to their wives, and divorce was quite common (though not as common as nowadays). A women could only obtain a divorce if her husband deserted her, though a man could divorce his wife for many reasons – if she produced no children, or simply if he grew tired of her. Some Romans – men as well as women – were critical of

Family life, as carved on tombs, was very important to the Romans, who regarded their ancestors with religious reverence and tried to keep their memory alive. They hoped to produce sons to continue the family line. Boys were considered grown-up at 14, girls at 12; they might marry any time after that.

Right: The chief
importance of Roman
women was their
management of the
household. The family
was, in a sense, a
miniature version of
the empire.

Far right: Upper-class
women spent a long
time making
themselves look
beautiful. They wore
their hair long, and
arranged it in any
number of different
ways.

this unequal treatment.

A divorced woman could, in certain circumstances, gain control of her own dowry – the money paid by her family when she was married. In fact there were many rich, single women in Rome.

In general, families had as many children as possible. One reason for this was that so many babies died for they lacked the medical care we have today. The old custom of allowing unwanted babies, usually girls, to die, became less common as time went on, but it was not illegal. The sad evidence of inscriptions on children's graves shows that most Roman parents loved their children. A vast number of children's toys have been found by archaeologists, including wooden and rag dolls, carved animals, dolls' houses, wheeled toys, hobby-horses, and so on.

Although we know a good deal about Roman family life, most of what we know comes from the households of well-off people. There are few records of what went on in the poor districts, where people could not afford stone-built tombs, or in the remote parts of the empire. However, the poor did sometimes manage to afford a tombstone, and inscriptions show that the dead person was a member of a loving family.

The main job of a woman was to be a good wife and mother, yet many women were to be found in ordinary jobs. Mostly they were typical "women's work", such as nursing, dressmaking or hairdressing, but there were also women shopkeepers, clerks, fishers, even doctors – though they were rare. Working women usually came from humble families – slaves or former slaves.

Education

Early schooling was the responsibility of mothers and nursemaids. Most girls and boys went to primary school at seven to learn reading and writing, but primary-school teachers were not much respected and most pupils were only taught to learn by heart, with frequent use of the cane. Intelligent Romans sometimes complained about these methods of teaching.

A smaller number of children went on to grammar school, where the main subject was literature – Greek, as well as Latin. A still smaller number of boys finished their education at a school of rhetoric. There they were taught the subjects necessary for a career in public service, such as public speaking and the ability to conduct a debate or legal argument. Most educated Roman citizens could speak Greek as well as they could speak Latin.

Young men from top families, who would be following a career in government, sometimes went on a "grand tour" of the empire. They went, not to primitive places like Britain, but to the old centres of Greek civilization: in Greece itself, Turkey, and, especially, Alexandria in Egypt, home of the ancient world's greatest library.

A teacher and his pupils at an elementary school, where children were taught the basics of reading, writing and arithmetic.

Food and Drink

In the days of the early Roman Republic, people ate simple meals. Under the emperors, those who could afford it became decidedly greedy. Breakfast and lunch remained simple, but the evening meal, which often began in the late afternoon, was an occasion for self-indulgence which, even by the standards of the rich today, seems slightly shocking. As everyone knows, the Romans would deliberately make themselves sick when they were full up in order to eat more.

One rich man's table was described (critically) by Varro in the 1st century B.C.: "Peacock from Samos, hazel hens from Phrygia, cranes from Media, young kids from Ambracia, tuna from Chalcedon, lampreys from Tartesus, white fish from Pessinus, oysters from Tarentum, scallops from Chios, swordfish from Rhodes, parrot fish from Cilicia, nuts from Thasos, dates from Egypt, acorns from Iberia – a truly imperial meal!"

Of course, not even the rich ate like that every day. More common was a three-course meal, including hors d'oeuvres (doormice were a favourite delicacy), followed by roast or boiled meat and a final course which might be shellfish or fruits and nuts. A good deal of wine was drunk as well.

People ate with knife and spoon – no forks – and as they ate while reclining on couches instead of sitting on chairs, they tended to use one hand only.

The poor, of course, knew nothing of this good living. Most of them had no kitchens anyway, though they could buy cheap hot dishes from take-aways. Others cooked on a small stove in the street. But bread was their staple diet.

Entertainment

Luxurious banquets were one form of entertainment, but the Romans had many

others, some of them exceedingly unpleasant. The Romans were so "civilized" in so many ways that their more brutal sports, such as throwing criminals to wild animals, are all the more shocking.

The Roman games once had a religious purpose, as a thanksgiving to the gods, but under the emperors their purpose became entirely political. They provided an outlet for the rebellious spirits of the Roman masses, and were the only occasions when all sections of the population came together.

Chariot racing was a popular – and dangerous – sport. It took place in the Circus Maximus, which held nearly 200,000 spectators. Four regular teams – White, Red, Green and Blue – took part. Fights between gladiators, and wild-beast shows, usually involving horrific bloodshed, took place in the Colosseum. The Emperor Commodus, who was mentally disturbed, once killed five crocodiles himself in one afternoon.

These were "popular" entertainments, which disgusted many intelligent Romans almost as much as they disgust us. There

Above: A banquet. The Romans liked to eat well, and the feasts of the later years of the empire set an extraordinary standard of greed.

Opposite: This baker, selling loaves or cakes in the open market, is pictured in a mosaic.

23

The Colosseum in Rome. The height to the top of the outer wall is nearly 50 m (164 ft), and the building measured 200 m by 160 m (218 × 175 yds). Built on the site of the "Golden House", the hugely extravagant palace of the Emperor Nero, it was only part of a vast building complex.

were, of course, more civilized forms of amusement, such as the theatre, where plays by Greek and Latin dramatists were performed.

Upper-class Romans also spent a lot of time at the public baths, but not just to wash. The actual baths were very elaborate and included steam baths, air baths, hot and cold baths and so on, and were a kind of social club. A man could take part in gymnastics, wrestling, have a massage, talk to his friends, eat and drink; some baths even had libraries. The famous baths of Caracalla, built about A.D. 250 (the ruins can still be seen), covered an area of about 30 acres.

Gladiators fought duels to the death to entertain the Romans. They were highly trained, like athletes, in gladiatorial schools, and specialized in different types of weapons and styles of fighting. One type, for example (the loser in this mosaic picture), fought with a net, a trident (a three-pronged spear) and dagger.

Work

Farming

Of all the possible ways of earning a living, said Cicero in the 1st century B.C., agriculture was the best, the most productive, and the most suitable for a free man. Cicero was thinking of well-to-do citizens like himself, who certainly never got their hands dirty in the fields; they had slaves to do the work. Still, he was right to say that farming was the most important occupation in the Roman Empire. We may think of the Romans as city people, but throughout the empire the land and its products were the foundation of Roman civilization.

Farms varied in size. There was a trend, especially in Italy, for rich men to build up very large estates, but in most other parts of the empire the typical farm was a one-family business.

In many areas Roman rule did not bring any changes to the life of ordinary people, but it did bring some improvements, such as better communications, leading to bigger markets, and better tools. Several books were written on the subject of farming which show a good deal of sound knowledge on matters like type of soil, fertilizers and drainage. In some parts experiments were made with crop rotation (growing different types of crop in successive seasons), which is more productive than the alternative of allowing the land to lie fallow every third or fourth year. The Romans also seem to have invented the coulter, the knife-like blade on a plough which cuts the ground ahead of the ploughshare.

Cereals were the main crop. Rome itself depended on Egypt for its supply of wheat. Barley – for animal fodder and beer-making – was widely grown on lighter soils, and oats in the north-western provinces. (It was the Romans who introduced oats – and therefore porridge – to Scotland.)

The main vegetables were various types of bean, including broad beans, as well as turnips. They provided winter fodder for animals as well as food for people. In gardens and small plots, lettuce, cabbage, radishes and asparagus were grown. Orchards produced peaches and apricots, apples and pears, plums and quinces, cherries, almonds and other nuts.

Two other crops were widely grown in Italy and the Mediterranean provinces: olives and grapes. Olive trees take a long time to bear fruit, but once they are established they need little attention. The crop was pressed to extract the oil, used mainly in cooking. Grapes were grown in almost every province, even chilly Britain. Most of the crop was trampled by human feet and the resulting juice fermented to make wine. Stored in large pottery jars, the wine was often kept for several years before it was drunk.

Sheep were kept mainly for their wool, but also for milk and cheese, though more

Below: An early "combine harvester", in which a scoop with sharp teeth was pushed into the growing wheat.

Below right: Grapes were grown widely to be made into wine. Artists, like those who made this mosaic in Roman Syria, were fond of showing the grapes being trampled in a vat. Wine was usually mixed with water before drinking, and sometimes with herbs and spices to make a kind of cocktail.

cheese came from goats. On some big estates, experiments were made in breeding sheep to get more milk. The Romans' favourite meat was pork, and pigs were kept all over the empire. They were easier to feed in the winter than most other farm animals, and could be driven into the forest to find their own food. Beef was less popular, and cows' milk was regarded as inferior to sheep's or goats'. Cattle, however, provided hides for leather, and oxen were the main working animals, drawing the plough and heavy carts, while donkeys did the lighter work and sometimes turned the millstones to grind the corn. Chickens were kept for their eggs and meat.

Trade and Tradesmen

The Roman Empire thrived on trade, which was probably the richest business after farming. One Roman writer, Juvenal, wrote early in the 2nd century A.D.: "The harbours and the sea are crowded with great ships. Already there are almost more men there than on the land..." (He was exaggerating of course.) Goods were always carried by water if possible because, in spite of the excellent roads, it was much cheaper. It cost more to transport goods 100 km by cart than to ship them the whole length of the Mediterranean Sea.

The main Roman exports were manufactures – metal goods, pottery, glass, etc. In return, Rome imported a good deal of food, notably grain from North Africa.

Trade reached beyond the frontiers of the empire. Rich Roman ladies wore tunics made of Chinese silk. Spices, costly woods like teak and precious stones (including diamonds) came from India. The discovery of the regular monsoon winds in the Indian Ocean enabled ships to sail direct from the Red Sea to India. Sailors usually preferred to stick close to the coast, even in the Mediterranean.

Merchants who took part in international trade were usually big businessmen, who had central offices and a chain of shops in Rome and other centres. But most business in the Roman Empire was on a small scale. Usually a craftsmen, like a baker, a cook or a silversmith, was also a retailer, selling his own products in his own shop. Even the big potteries of Arezzo, in central Italy, whose products have been found throughout the empire, employed only about 60 workmen (slaves).

Below left: Roman goldsmiths and silversmiths could win a high reputation by their skill. Their works included bowls decorated with portrait medallions, cups and scenes in relief, mirrors and various kinds of ornament. Rich Romans paid enormous prices for such art objects. This is part of the Mildenhall treasure in the British Museum, which was probably buried to foil robbers in the 4th century A.D.

Below: This marble relief sculpture from Pompeii shows a smith's workshop. The metal being worked is copper, and the smith is surrounded by his family. The older boys are already learning their father's trade.

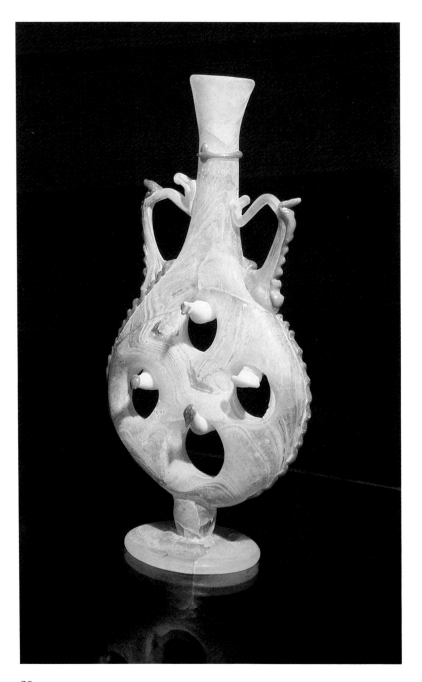

Of all the objects made in workshops of the Roman Empire which have survived to find their final resting place in a modern museum, perhaps the most impressive are glass vessels. It is something of a miracle that objects so fragile should have survived at all. The main reason is that glass vessels containing offerings were often placed inside stone coffins, remaining undisturbed for many centuries.

The technique of blowing glass was discovered in the 1st century B.C., probably in Syria, and in less than 100 years blown-glass vessels were being made as far away as northern France and Belgium. Glass-makers were extraordinarily skilful at every glassmaking technique, and fine examples often bear the maker's name. At least one, Sentia Secunda, was a woman.

The type of work a person does is also a measure of his importance in society: rightly or wrongly, we regard doctors more highly than cleaners. The Romans were no different. Cicero described the social rank of different jobs in the 1st century B.C. Certain occupations, he wrote, are generally disliked. These include tax collectors and moneylenders. All unskilled work is low-class, and not fit for a free man, because such work is simply that of a paid slave. Middlemen, who buy goods from a dealer and re-sell them at a profit, are despised. Anyone who works in a trade is also low-class, but certain trades, especially those which cater to people's greed (butchers, fishmongers, cooks, etc) are 'lower' than others. Cicero also classes with these "actors, dancers and the whole pack of low-grade performers". Professions, which required a more serious approach, such as medicine, architecture and teaching, are much more respectable. A small trader is low-class, but a merchant with a large business, dealing with goods on an international scale, is more acceptable, if only because such a man usually invests his money in land and thus becomes – Cicero's ideal – a landed gentleman.

Opposite: A glass flask made in the ingenious form of a dovecote, about 250 A.D. The Romans were especially fond of luxuriously coloured glass, and the techniques of glassmakers were extremely advanced.

This piece of Roman glassware, known as the Portland Vase after a previous owner, is now in the British Museum. Made in the early 1st century A.D., it consists of two layers, white and blue. The outer layer was cut away to make the picture with the aid of grinding wheels, tiny chisels and gravers. It has been smashed twice in recent times, but carefully restored by the Museum's craftsmen.

1079. SOLDATS PRÉTORIENS
Rome   II.ᵉ siècle ap. J.-C.

The Praetorian Guard was the most privileged section of the army, paid three times as much as ordinary soldiers and stationed near Rome. Anyone who hoped to become emperor had to have the support of this force – the imperial bodyguard.

The Army

The power of Rome depended on its army. In the earlier years of the Republic, fighting was everybody's business, and the army was simply all the men in the state who were fit to fight. But empires are not easily won by part-time soldiers, and even if they are won, they are not kept for centuries. The army commanded by Julius Caesar was a highly professional one. Its soldiers were trained men, hardened by months of drill, who had signed on for twenty years. They were volunteers for whom the army offered a good career, with regular wages and the chance of booty seized from defeated enemies. At the end of their service, if they survived (about half did not), they might receive land and a house in a new provincial town, as well as a retirement bonus equal to about twelve years' wages. While serving, they were also compelled to save a proportion of their pay – a kind of National Insurance system.

In the 1st century A.D. about 150,000 Romans, mostly from peasant families, served in the army, which was divided into about 30 legions. Each legion contained 60 "centuries" – companies of (in theory) 100 men, though usually less. The centurions, commanders of a century, were the core of the army. An ordinary legionary, if he did well, could expect to reach centurion's rank before the end of his service.

On campaign, there were usually many non-Roman allies attached to the army, like the Numidian cavalry or the Balearic slingers. As time went on, even the legions became increasingly non-Italian, though as Roman soldiers, the men also became Roman citizens.

The cream of the army was the Praetorian Guard, who were recruited only in Italy. They were stationed near Rome and were better paid than ordinary legionaries, besides receiving extra payments from time to time from the emperor, who was always careful to keep their support. Anyone with designs on the imperial title first made sure of winning the support of the Praetorian Guard.

Legionaries spent many years on guard duty in distant provinces, where many of them eventually settled. Their links with Rome were therefore rather weak, and their first loyalty was given not to 'the Senate and People', nor even to the emperor, but to their own generals. It was chiefly this loyalty which caused the civil wars that ended the Republic and, in later times, sometimes decided who should be the next emperor.

Under the *pax Romana*, the legionaries spent more time stationed in camps near frontiers or on guard duty elsewhere than fighting campaigns. In those circumstances, the army expanded to include a horde of people who far outnumbered the actual soldiers. These included women and even children, as well as hangers-on of the kind who attach themselves to any army. There was also a large staff, consisting of clerks, engineers, surveyors, priests, doctors, vets and others.

This coin of Republican Rome shows on one side a galley – a large boat driven by oars, carrying soldiers across the sea. The Romans were not great sailors by nature, and when they had to cross water they preferred, if possible, to build a bridge.

According to the historian Josephus, "Roman soldiers are as quick to act as they are slow to give way, and there was never a battle in which they were defeated by superior numbers, by tactical skill or unfavourable ground, or even by fortune, which they could command less easily than military supremacy." The Roman army had a formidable reputation. But what made the Romans such a great military power was not that they won every battle – they lost some even at the height of their power – but that they seldom lost a campaign. Their greatest military quality was discipline. They were often savage, but they never panicked and they never fled.

Like all armies, the Roman army had weaknesses as well as strengths. In a pitched battle its discipline, tactics, training and weaponry made the Roman infantry almost invincible. By comparison, the cavalry was weak. The Romans were not natural horsemen, and they were less effective in a fast-moving situation, against lighter-armed troops, or in guerilla warfare. In those circumstances, when they were unable to confront the enemy in a pitched battle, the Romans carried out a calculated policy of terror, including sometimes the massacre of civilians, as well as the destruction of crops and settlements.

Armour naturally changed over the centuries, but legionaries normally wore a bronze or iron helmet which also protected cheeks and neck, and they carried a rectangular shield, guarding them from throat to knees, which was made of several thin layers of wood, bound in leather with metal fittings. In later times they wore a tunic of chain-mail or plate armour over their tunics. Aggressive weapons consisted of two throwing spears, one heavy, one light, and – the main weapon for close-quarters fighting – a shortish, broad, double-edged sword, as well as a dagger. As they had to construct camps and build roads and defenceworks, they also had a lot of other equipment to carry on the march. They paid for their own equipment out of their wages.

Greaves, guarding the lower leg, were worn by centurions, who also had grander helmets. Centurions carried a baton or stick, which they sometimes used to beat their men. The commander of a legion, who was often a senator serving his spell in the army on his way up the political ladder, was grander still, his cloak and armour often being specially made to his own design.

On the move, the army was an impressive, not to say terrifying sight, a blaze of colour with each unit carrying identical shields and a standard-bearer marching in front of each legion and century. Conquered tribes, watching this display, thought very hard before staging a rebellion.

In the end, of course, the Romans lost. The frontiers of the empire were too long to be guarded effectively against the fierce, fast-riding "barbarians" who threatened it at so many points. Distant provinces, like Britain, had to be abandoned; the defences caved in and, in the end, Rome itself fell.

Roman soldiers on the attack. At close quarters their main weapon was the short sword. But the main reasons for their success were training and discipline.

Buildings

The success of the Roman army was due not only to its fighting qualities but also to its engineers and surveyors. As heavy weapons could not be carried on a long march, the Romans constructed their "war machines" on the spot. The "artillery" consisted of two main types. One type was basically a gigantic bow fixed on a heavy wooden base and operated by a winch. It could fire missiles like huge arrows, or stones. The second type worked more like a catapult, with a rope made of some elastic material like animal sinew. One of these machines, used when the Romans were besieging Jerusalem, could hurl a stone ball weighing over 20 kg (42 lbs) a distance of 400 metres (437 yards).

Other war machines included the ram – a large, wooden, metal-ended spike for smashing through city gates – and various ingenious defences against cavalry, such as iron hooks fixed in concealed logs.

Surviving examples of Roman bridges, like this one in Turkey, display qualities characteristic of nearly all Roman building: strength and dignity. As they did not have the theoretical knowledge of today's engineers, the Roman builders erred on the side of safety, making their bridges stronger than they needed to be.

Bridges and Aqueducts

The army forded rivers when possible, sometimes using boats, but this was regarded as a slightly second-rate solution. Romans preferred to build bridges, which demonstrated their mastery over water as well as land. They hammered in wooden piles and built a frame-work of treetrunks, filling in with bundles of sticks bound together. Julius Caesar reported that one such bridge was finished ten days after the men began cutting down trees for it.

Permanent bridges were usually built of stone, or stone and wood, and "permanent" is no exaggeration for some of these bridges are still standing. Under the Emperor Trajan (A.D. 98–117) a bridge was built across the Danube in what is now Rumania which was carried on 20 stone piers, each 40 m (44 yards) high and 20 m (22 yards) wide, standing 50 m (55 yards) apart. The actual bridge which rested on the piers was made of wood.

The skill of the Romans as construction engineers was most often shown in the building of aqueducts, or waterways. A good water supply is a vital necessity for any town, especially a Roman town where the liking for frequent bathing had to be considered. Rivers and wells could not always supply enough, and in some places water had to be brought from a long distance.

An aqueduct – or a bridge for that matter – was expensive. Several neighbouring towns might get together to pay for a bridge which would benefit all of them, and if a

The remains of several aqueducts still stand, evidence of the Romans' determination to overcome any difficulties Nature put in their way. This is the famous Pont du Garde in the south of France, which is 2,000 years old.

town could not afford an aqueduct, it might be paid for by a rich citizen, or even by the emperor himself. A surveyor, often one attached to the army, was employed to plan its construction.

The best source of water was a mountain spring, from which water would flow downhill, perhaps for several miles, to the town. It travelled through stone channels, or through pipes made of lead or earthenware. An aqueduct would be necessary to carry it across low ground or valleys, and tunnels might have to be dug if there were large hills between the source and the town. When it reached the town, the water was stored in tanks near the walls, and pipes carried it to the public baths, fountains and other buildings, including some private houses of wealthier citizens. Some aqueducts carried a road along the top as well as the water channel.

Rome had no less than 14 large aqueducts bringing fresh spring water from the Apennine Mountains to the city. It was stored in about 250 reservoirs, and modern experts have calculated that the rate of supply was almost 1 billion litres (220 million gallons) a day.

The Romans were a practical and hygienic people and nothing illustrates that better than their drains and sewers, which were not equalled in Europe until the 19th century. An extensive drainage system was built in republican Rome, some remains of which can be seen today. The vaulted, underground channels that carried the waste away to the River Tiber were about 5 m ($5\frac{1}{2}$ yards) wide.

As a rule, only the houses of rich Romans were directly connected to the water supply, via lead pipes, but the ground floors of some big apartment blocks may also have had their own supply.

Roman villas also had a form of central heating (rare in British houses until about 1950!). Warm air, heated by a furnace, passed under the floors and through hollow bricks in the walls.

Roads

Roman roads are famous, and in many countries modern roads still follow the original Roman route. For the Romans built better roads in Europe than anyone else did until about 200 years ago. They were mainly built for – and by – the army, and their most notable quality is that they were amazingly straight (though not always as straight as people think; the Romans were not fools and did not build a road straight up and over a hill if it were easier to go round it). For marching soldiers, the shorter the route the better, and the Romans did not have to worry much about building through private property.

A Roman poet, Statius, described how a road was built in about 100 A.D. First, furrows were marked out for a deep trench. The trench was dug and filled with sand and small stones as a foundation. The heavy paving stones which formed the surface of the road were held in place by kerbs and, if necessary, wedges. Not all roads were paved, of course. Minor routes, and roads in places like North Africa where the ground was dry and hard, were sandy tracks.

Roads were built one Roman mile (1,000 marching paces, or 1,481 metres) at a time. Each mile was marked by a milestone in the form of a short pillar, on which was written the distance from the nearest town, together with the name of the reigning emperor. It is sometimes possible to detect a slight change in the line of the road where a new mile begins.

Although the Romans had maps, they were not very accurate ones. A traveller would rely on a list of places along the road, which gave the mileage between them.

Even roads built for the army were naturally used by many other travellers, such as merchants and public officials. The Emperor Augustus organized a postal system, using relays of fresh horses kept at intervals along the road, so that official despatches could travel as quickly as possible.

Roads spanned the
empire. Though
mostly built for speedy
movement of troops,
they served as
Europe's main
highways for many
centuries. This is the
Via Appia, or Appian
Way, near Rome.

Public Buildings

The Romans were the heirs of Greek civilization, but it would be wrong to think that they simply copied Greek ideas, in architecture or in anything else. The Roman genius was for engineering and practical experiment; the Greeks were their superiors in their appreciation of beauty, but were far behind them in technique. Greek and Roman temples may at first look rather alike, yet in some fundamental ways Greek and Roman architecture were completely different.

Greek buildings are founded on straight lines; Roman buildings make more use of rounded shapes, like the arch, the vault (rounded roof) and the dome. In Greek buildings, the most important element is the column, while in Roman buildings it is usually the walls which are the essential elements in the structure. Columns in roman buildings are sometimes merely ornamental. A building like the Maison Carrée at Nîmes in the south of France has a porch with columns at each end, but on the sides the columns are "engaged" (attached) to the walls which support the roof.

Style in architecture is determined to a large extent by the materials and techniques available to the builders. What made it possible for the Romans to build domes and vaults was their invention of concrete. Their domes were built of brick and concrete (which was also economical because builder's waste could be used to mix with the cement). The visible surfaces were given a facing of plaster or marble.

Concrete domes were built in the 2nd century B.C. if not earlier. There was one on the public baths at Pompeii, a city which has been preserved as a result of the eruption of Mount Vesuvius, which buried it in ash in A.D. 79.

Perhaps the most magnificent building of ancient Rome, which is also a miraculous feat of engineering, is the Pantheon, a temple built by the Emperor Hadrian in the early 2nd century A.D. Its dome is 43 metres

Above: The Roman temple known as the Maison Carrée at Nîmes, the best preserved of all Roman temples. It was built in the time of the Emperor Augustus. Like most Roman temples, it stands on a high base, or podium, and shows Etruscan as well as Greek influence.

Left: The public baths (like those at Pompeii) were not just for keeping clean. They were also a social and sports club, among other things. There was a small admission charge, which ensured that the poorer citizens did not use them too often.

(47 yards) across – larger than St. Paul's in London. Measurement of the Pantheon has revealed a subtle plan: the building is based on the form of a sphere or circle, the height of the supporting walls being exactly the same as the radius of the dome.

One of the most typical Roman buildings was the basilica, a large, oblong meeting hall with rows of columns inside, like a Greek temple turned inside out. The earliest Christian churches were built on this pattern, but no one in the West built domes like the Romans until over a thousand years later.

The Romans are remembered for several other types of building, such as public baths, which were often richly decorated with sculpture and painting, and amphitheatres, of which the Colosseum in Rome was the largest. Another characteristic Roman building was the triumphal arch, a great stone gateway which was usually built as a monument to the military achievements of some emperor or general. They were decorated with inscriptions and battle scenes carved into the stone. A famous example is the Arch of Titus, built to celebrate the conquest of Jerusalem in A.D. 70 (A modern example of course, is the famous Arc de Triomphe in Paris).

Religion

Roman Gods

In the earliest times, the religion of the Romans was the typical religion of simple farmers, in which spirits or powers inhabited everything in Nature – stones, trees, waterfalls, etc. These spirits had to be kept friendly by sacrifices and ceremonies.

The most powerful Roman god was Jupiter, who became the chief god of the state. Other important gods included Minerva (goddess of crafts and wisdom), Mars (god of war and farm work) and Neptune (god of the sea). There were many more, and as time went by a great number of foreign gods were adopted by the Romans. The old gods became identified with others, especially the gods of ancient Greece. Thus Jupiter was Zeus, Minerva was Athena, Mars was Ares, etc. The Romans also worshipped ideas, such as "virtue", "honour" and so on.

Minor, local gods included family gods, the *manes* (spirits of dead ancestors), the *lares* who inhabited a particular place and had shrines at crossroads, and the *penates*, gods of the household.

The gods made their will known through signs or omens. Before an important political or military event, attempts were made to discover the will of the gods (or, what was going to happen) from signs in the sky, like the flight of birds, or by examining the insides of a slaughtered animal.

The gods were kept in a good mood by prayers and sacrifices. The historian Livy, who lived in the time of Augustus, believed that Rome's success was the result of correctly observing the will of the gods. "Those who followed the gods had every success", he wrote, "while those who disregarded them met with misfortune."

Religion and politics were closely connected. If you did not observe the state religion you were unpatriotic, if not worse. Politicians often held a priestly office.

Julius Caesar, despite being an atheist, was at one time the chief priest.

By Caesar's time, however, religion had changed. That foreign religions were so easily accepted shows that people were dissatisfied with traditional Roman religion. In country districts, beliefs had probably not changed greatly, but among intelligent Roman citizens there was less and less

Opposite, left: The Temple of Jupiter at Baalbek, in Syria.

Opposite, below: A relief from the Arch of Titus in Rome.

Below: Roman statue of Jupiter.

The Emperor Marcus Aurelius conducts a sacrifice on the Capitol in Rome.

The Imperial Cult

Augustus was also responsible for encouraging the imperial cult – the worship of the emperor as a god. The idea of a divine ruler was quite familiar in eastern provinces, but it was new in Europe. However, the imperial cult was never forced on the whole empire in a single form. It was adapted to local circumstances and, not surprisingly, it was stronger in the east. Not too much was made of it in Rome, where Augustus always spoke of himself as merely the first among equals.

In other words, the imperial cult was also essentially political. It helped to increase the authority of the emperor, and therefore to keep the empire loyal and devoted. On the simplest level, people were less likely to rebel against a god than a mere man!

belief in the gods of Rome. Astrology became fashionable, which is often a sign of religious decline.

Deep religious feelings were still there, however, and the civil war that followed the death of Caesar was seen by many people as a punishment from the gods.

This set the stage for the restoration of Roman religion by Augustus. Under his rule, ruined temples were rebuilt, priests were appointed to offices which had long remained vacant, forgotten ceremonies were revived, and the Emperor himself took a leading part in religious worship. Augustus realized better than anyone that religion was political. It was part of the framework which held Roman civilization together.

However, although Augustus could rebuild temples and order religious services to be held, he could not change people's beliefs. The old Roman gods were still unsatisfactory, and the way was still open for the growth of stronger religions that had a greater appeal.

Right: The Emperor Augustus, a cameo of the 1st century A.D. His firm, but generally wise rule, put an end to the civil wars which marked the collapse of the Republic.

Other religions

The liveliest religions of the Roman Empire were the "mystery" cults. Although the Roman rulers, always on the lookout for plots, regarded them with suspicion, there was no religious bias against them. It was only the air of secrecy which aroused distrust, and the worship of Isis, originally an Egyptian goddess, and of Cybele, the "Great Mother", became very popular, especially with women.

Mithraism was especially popular among soldiers. It was a very masculine kind of religion based on the belief that Mithras himself was a go-between of gods and men, who had ascended to heaven after killing a mythical bull from whose blood all life sprang. The religion came originally from Iran. The legionaries carried it all over the empire: a temple to Mithras has been discovered in London.

The Roman rulers were willing to tolerate all religions as long as they were not a threat. As long as the worshippers of Mithras or Isis also recognized the official religion, they were accepted. One of the new religions, however, was different.

Christians insisted that their god was the only god, and that to worship other gods (including the emperor) was sinful. Christianity threatened the whole political-religious establishment, and it is therefore not surprising that Christians in Rome were persecuted. As everyone knows, some of them were fed to the lions in the Colosseum.

In fact, Christians were only fiercely persecuted at certain periods, for instance under the Emperor Nero. Moreover, persecution did not check the growth of Christianity. In fact the herosim of Christian martyrs encouraged the faith.

Christianity made a powerful appeal to people's emotions in a way that the vague and garbled religious traditions of Rome had long ceased to do. And it was stronger than Mithraism, its chief rival, because it appealed to men and women alike.

Head of the god Mithras, from Arles in southern France. Mithraism was spread throughout the empire by the army, and it is easy to see why Mithras, the tough, unconquerable hero, appealed so much to soldiers.

In the end, Christianity triumphed. The Emperor Constantine (A.D. 306–337) made it the official religion of the empire, and it was to have a greater effect on the future of Europe than even the Roman tradition. Soon, emperors would cease to rule Rome. But Rome remained the residence of another sort of ruler – the Pope, head of the Church, who is still there.

A magnificent gold coin of the Emperor Constantine. Bronze and silver coins were in use in Rome by about 300 B.C. The main coin was the silver *denarius*. Gold coins were introduced by Julius Caesar, whose portrait appeared on them; this was normal under the emperors. Roman coins are sometimes turned up nowadays by farmers, gardeners, or even children.

Literature and the Arts

The great intellectual achievements of the Roman Empire mostly came, not from Rome, but from Greek cities, especially from the Greeks of Alexandria. It is a mark of the intelligence of the Romans that they recognized the superior quality of the older Greek civilization in many respects.

Greek superiority lay in things of the mind and the spirit. In more practical affairs, the Romans were far advanced, but abstract ideas did not come easily to them. They regarded the great Greek philosophers of the past almost as magicians or semi-religious prophets. Roman knowledge of science and medicine was considerable, but most of it came from the Greeks.

The huge and famous work on *Natural History* by Pliny the Elder (a true scientist — he was killed when he went too close while observing the eruption of Mount Vesuvius) was certainly a great work. But it was largely copied from Greek works. There were no Romans in the 2nd century A.D. who could be compared with Ptolemy (an Alexandrian) on geography and astronomy, or with Galen (from the Greek city of Pergamum in Asia Minor) on human anatomy. The famous Greek inventor, Archimedes, was killed by a Roman soldier who did not know who he was while he was working out a geometrical problem in the sand with a stick.

Yet, despite the unfortunate death of Archimedes, the Greek intellectuals of Alexandria and other places would not have flourished but for the *pax Romana*.

Wax tablets and stylus, or "pen". Corrections could be made easily by rubbing out and smoothing the layer of wax with the blunt end of the stylus. The Romans also wrote with ink made from various substances such as cuttlefish and soot on papyrus sheets (made from pressed reeds) and later parchment (animal skin).

Language and Literature

Latin, as befitted a people like the Romans, is a very practical language. In the West, it became the common language of educated people for over a thousand years – a greater gift to European civilization than stone monuments. Latin is a strong and logical language in which the variations of nouns and verbs (cases, tenses, etc.) are achieved by changing the endings of the words, instead of using a number of extra words, as in English or French. It is not a particularly easy language to learn, but it is neat, clear, forceful, and surprisingly flexible.

It was also a language capable of being made into great literature. The Romans did not produce tragic playwrights of quite the same powerful genius as Sophocles or Euripides, and perhaps Virgil's *Aeneid* affects us less strongly than Homer's *Iliad* and *Odyssey* (which were Virgil's models). Nevertheless, Virgil was a great poet, and there were many others, Catullus, Horace, Ovid among them.

Roman prose reached its peak in the work of Cicero. Later came, among others, Livy and Tacitus, the historians; Seneca, the tragedian; Pliny, the scientist; Martial and Juvenal, the sharp-tongued satirists; and Apuleius, the novelist who wrote *The Golden Ass*.

The Roman theatre at Orange in the south of France, looking towards the stage from the auditorium.

43

Painting and Sculpture

In the arts as well as in literature and architecture, truly Roman products took a long time to develop because the Romans originally took over the artistic ideas of the Greeks and the Etruscans, their former rulers.

Ancestor worship provided the motive for the development of portraits – in painting and sculpture – which were almost unknown in Classical Greece. If we have to think of a typical Roman artwork, we probably think of a marble bust of a Roman patrician, very lifelike yet displaying the virtues of strength, honour and devotion to duty which the Romans regarded so highly.

Tombs and monuments were decorated with relief sculpture. The finest surviving example in Rome is Trajan's Column, showing 155 scenes of the Emperor's achievements in a spiral band about 200 metres (219 yards) long. Often, however, the historical interest of such works is greater than their artistic value.

The Romans eagerly collected Greek works of art; according to Pliny the Elder, Rome was packed with them, and when Greek originals grew scarce, Roman art lovers had copies made (often by Greek craftsmen). It is through Roman copies that we know of many of the most famous works of the Classical Greek sculptors, such as Myron's discus thrower.

Roman and Greek sculpture is mainly familiar to us in old bronze or marble. This gives a misleading impression of what, say, a temple full of statues really looked like. Originally, the statues were coloured, and inset with glass eyes and other details.

By the end of the 2nd century A.D., new forms of expression had appeared in Roman art, in which the idealistic quality of Greece gave way to more lively and emotional works, especially in portraits.

Paintings do not last as well as sculpture, but as a result of the tragic volcanic eruption which buried the towns of Pompeii and Herculaneum, the gorgeous wall paintings

that decorated private homes, as well as palaces and other buildings, can be seen today almost as they were nearly 2,000 years ago.

Archaeologists have also discovered many of the fine mosaics that were used for floors, and later for walls and ceilings. There are fine examples to be seen in the large Roman villa at Fishbourne in Sussex. For such work to be found in so distant a province as Britain demonstrates the remarkable spread of the finest works of Rome throughout the empire.

Above: Roman villas were richly decorated.

Left: The Discus Thrower, a copy of a Classical Greek statue in bronze by Myron.

Opposite: Trajan's Column illustrates the wars in Dacia in the early 2nd century A.D.

Index

Figures in *italics* refer to captions.